Alikira Richard

Job Satisfaction from Herzberg's Two Factor Theory Perspective

Der GRIN Verlag publiziert seit 1998 wissenschaftliche Arbeiten von Studenten, Hochschullehrern und anderen Akademikern als eBook und gedrucktes Buch. Die Verlagswebsite www.grin.com ist die ideale Plattform zur Veröffentlichung von Hausarbeiten, Abschlussarbeiten, wissenschaftlichen Aufsätzen, Dissertationen und Fachbüchern.

Alikira Richard

Job Satisfaction from Herzberg's Two Factor Theory Perspective

GRIN Verlag

Die Deutsche Bibliothek verzeichnet diese Publikation in der Deutschen Nationalbibliografie; detaillierte bibliografische Daten sind im Internet über http://dnb.d-nb.de/ abrufbar.

1. Auflage 2012
Copyright © 2012 GRIN Verlag GmbH
http://www.grin.com
Druck und Bindung: Books on Demand GmbH, Norderstedt Germany
ISBN 978-3-656-35630-1

Job Satisfaction from Herzberg's Two Factor Theory Point of View

Contents

Introduction

According to Suzan M, heartfield, Employee satisfaction is a terminology used to describe whether employees are happy and contented and fulfilling their desires and needs at work. Many measures purport that employee satisfaction is a factor in employee motivation, employee goal achievement, and positive employee morale in the workplace. Whereas job satisfaction is generally positive the organization's success, it can also be a downer if mediocre employees stay because they are satisfied with your work environment. Several factors including; treating employees with respect, providing regular employee recognition, empowering employees, offering above industry-average benefits and compensation, providing employee perks and company activities, and positive management within a success framework of goals, measurements, and expectations all contribute to an employee's level of satisfaction. Employee satisfaction is looked at in areas such as: management, understanding of mission and vision, empowerment, teamwork, communication, and coworker interaction.

Some of the signs of lack of employee satisfaction are high levels of absenteeism and staff turnover and can affect the organization's bottom line, as recruitment and retraining take their toll. But few organizations have made job satisfaction a top priority, perhaps because they have failed to understand the significant opportunity that lies in front of them.

Satisfied employees on the other hand tend to be more productive, creative and committed to their employers, and recent studies have shown a direct correlation between staff satisfaction and their performance. For example, employers who can create work environments that attract, motivate and retain hard-working individuals will be better positioned to succeed in a competitive environment that demands quality and

cost-efficiency. In fact, employers may even discover that by creating a positive workplace for their employees, they increase their own job satisfaction as well.

The Herzberg's two factor theory

In the late 1950s, Frederick Herzberg, considered by many to be a pioneer in motivation theory, interviewed a group of employees to find out what made them satisfied and dissatisfied on the job. He asked the employees essentially two sets of questions:

1. Think of a time when you felt especially good about your job. Why did you feel that way?
2. Think of a time when you felt especially bad about your job. Why did you feel that way?

From these interviews Herzberg went on to develop his theory that there are two dimensions to job satisfaction: motivation and "hygiene". Hygiene issues, according to Herzberg, cannot motivate employees but can minimize dissatisfaction, if handled properly. In other words, they can only dissatisfy if they are absent or mishandled. Hygiene topics include company policies, supervision, salary, interpersonal relations and working conditions. They are issues related to the employee's environment. Motivators, on the other hand, create satisfaction by fulfilling individuals' needs for meaning and personal growth. They are issues such as achievement, recognition, the work itself, responsibility and advancement. Once the hygiene areas are addressed, said Herzberg, the motivators will promote job satisfaction and encourage production.

Two dimensions of employee satisfaction

Frederick Herzberg theorized that employee satisfaction depends on two sets of issues: "hygiene" issues and motivators. Once the hygiene issues have been addressed, he said, the motivators create satisfaction among employees.

Hygiene issues (dissatisfiers)	Motivators (satisfiers
Company and administrative policies	Work itself
Supervision	Achievement
Salary	Recognition
Interpersonal relations	Responsibility
Working conditions	Advancement

Determinants of job satisfaction

Determinants of job satisfaction can be derived from this very theory by examining its significance.

To apply Herzberg's theory to real-world practice, let us begin with the hygiene issues. Although hygiene issues are not the source of satisfaction, these issues must be dealt with first to create an environment in which employee satisfaction and motivation are even possible.

Company and administrative policies; An organization's policies can be a great source of frustration for most employees if the policies are unclear or unnecessary or if not everyone is required to follow them. Although employees will never feel a great sense of motivation or satisfaction due to organizational policies, employers can decrease dissatisfaction in this area by making sure that policies are fair and apply equally to all stakeholders. Managers should policies and procedures accessible to all members of staff. If you do not have a written manual, create one, soliciting staff input along the way.

Supervision; To decrease dissatisfaction in this area, you must begin by making wise decisions when you appoint someone to the role of supervisor. Be aware that good employees do not always make good supervisors. The role of supervisor is extremely difficult. It requires leadership skills and the ability to treat all employees fairly.

Supervisors need to use positive feedback whenever possible and should establish means of employee evaluation and feedback so that no one feels singled out.

Salary; although salary appears a motivator like the old saying "you get what you pay for", Salary is not a motivator for employees, but they do want to be paid fairly. If individuals believe they are not compensated well, they will be unhappy working for you. Consultation with other similar organizations to what employees are paid is very important in reducing job dissatisfaction. In addition, make sure you have clear policies related to salaries, raises and bonuses.

Interpersonal relations; Remember that part of the satisfaction of being employed is the social contact it brings, so allow employees a reasonable amount of time for socialization for example, over lunch, during breaks, introduce games e.t.c. This will help them develop a sense of camaraderie and teamwork. At the same time, you should crack down on rudeness, inappropriate behavior and offensive comments. If an individual continues to be disruptive, take charge of the situation, perhaps by dismissing him or her from the practice.

Working conditions; The environment in which people work has a tremendous effect on their level of pride for themselves and for the work they are doing. Do everything you can to keep your equipment and facilities up to date. Even a nice chair can make a world of difference to an individual's psyche. Also, if possible, avoid overcrowding and allow each employee his or her own personal space, whether it be a desk, a locker, or even just a drawer. If you overcrowd employees, with little or no personal space, don't be surprised that there is tension among them.

Thus there is need to remember that hygiene factors are not direct satisfiers they affect job satisfaction indirectly and failure to tackle them appropriately would be asking for trouble in more than one way. First, your employees would be generally unhappy, second, your hardworking employees, who can find jobs elsewhere, would leave, while

your mediocre employees would stay and compromise your working conditions. So deal with hygiene issues first, then move on to the motivators.

When employees are motivated, they get satisfied with their jobs as well Aswanthapa (2007). There several factors that determine job satisfaction and they comprise Herzberg's motivational factors.

The Work itself; as Suzan M heartfield a human resource guru once wrote "for an employee to be motivated, the job itself must be satisfying". Perhaps most important to employee motivation is helping individuals believe that the work they are doing is important and that their tasks are meaningful. Emphasize that their contributions to the practice result in positive outcomes .Share stories of success about how an employee's actions made a real difference in making a process better. Make a big deal out of meaningful tasks that may have become ordinary, such as increase in production. Of course employees may not find all their tasks interesting or rewarding, but you should show the employee how those tasks are essential to the overall processes that make the company succeed. Managers should identify certain tasks that are truly unnecessary and can be eliminated or streamlined, resulting in greater efficiency and satisfaction.

Achievement; One foundation inherent in Herzberg's theory is that most individuals sincerely want to do a good job. To help them, managers need to allocate/place employees in positions that use their talents and are not set up for failure. Set clear, achievable goals and standards for each position, and make sure employees know what those goals and standards are. Individuals should also receive regular, timely feedback on how they are doing and should feel they are being adequately challenged in their jobs. Be careful, however, not to overload individuals with challenges that are too difficult or impossible, as that can be paralyzing.

Recognition; Individuals at all levels of the organization want to be recognized for their achievements on the job. Their successes do not have to be monumental before they deserve recognition, but your praise should be sincere. If you notice employees

doing something well, take the time to acknowledge their good work immediately. Publicly thank them for handling a situation particularly well. Write them a kind note of praise or give them a bonus, if appropriate. You may even want to establish a formal recognition program, such as employee of the month or even of the week to create a platform on which to motivate your employees.

Responsibility; Employees will be more motivated to do their jobs well if they have ownership of their work. This requires giving employees enough freedom and power to carry out their tasks so that they feel they "own" the result. As individuals mature in their jobs, provide opportunities for added responsibility. Be careful, however, that you do not simply add more work. Instead, find ways to add challenging and meaningful work, perhaps giving the employee greater freedom and authority as well.

Advancement; Reward loyalty and performance with advancement. If you do not have an open position to which to promote a valuable employee, consider giving him or her a new title that reflects the level of work he or she has achieved. When feasible, support employees by allowing them to pursue further education, which will make them more valuable to your practice and more fulfilled professionally.

To evaluate your practice's performance in the area of job satisfaction and to identify where you might focus your efforts, complete the following self-assessment, which is structured around Frederick Herzberg's motivation-"hygiene" theory. As you answer each question, keep in mind the needs and concerns of your employees and colleagues.

Conclusion

While there is no one right way to manage people, all of whom have different needs, backgrounds and expectations; Herzberg's theory offers a reasonable starting point. By creating an environment that promotes job satisfaction, and for developing employees who are motivated, productive and fulfilled. Thus, Employee satisfaction affects every aspect of an employee, from his/her satisfaction to overall productivity and Frederick Herzberg theorized that employee satisfaction has two dimensions: "hygiene" and motivation. Hygiene issues, such as salary and supervision, decrease employees' dissatisfaction with the work environment. While motivators, such as recognition and achievement, make workers more productive, creative and committed.

References

Aswanthapa, k, (2007). *Human Resource management* (10th Ed.).New Delhi

Herzberg, F., Mausner, B., Snyderman, B. (1993). The Motivation to Work Somerset, NJ: Transaction Publishers; 1993.

Management of Organizational Behavior: Utilizing Human Resources, 7th ed. P. Hersey, K.H. Blanchard, D.E. Johnson. Upper Saddle River, NJ: Prentice-Hall; 1996.

Spector, P. (1997). *Job Satisfaction: Application, Assessment, Causes and Consequences* Thousand Oaks, Calif: SAGE Publications.

Syptak, M. (1998). Altruism in Practice Management: Caring for Your Staff. *Family Practice Management.* October 1998(1)58–60.

http://humanresources.about.com/od/employeesurvey1/g/employee_satisfy.htm